No Cats Have Been Maimed or Mutilated During the Making of this Book

...But Some of Them Are Disappointed — DEEPLY Disappointed — in Me

by Dean Blehert

Illustrations by Pam Coulter Blehert

Words & Pictures Press
Tustin, CA

This book is dedicated to Sally, Fred, Sam, Jenny and Cat — and especially to Sally, because she is watching my pen move now and may intervene if I don't give her some attention NOW.

Designed by Maggy Graham. Published by Words & Pictures Press, 18002 Irvine Blvd., Suite 200, Tustin, CA 92780, 714-544-7282.

ISBN No. 0-9644857-5-3
Library of Congress Catalog Card Number 96-60834

Introduction

Many of the poems in this book were previously printed in my "poetry letter," *Deanotations*, which, for 12 years, has gone out every two months to a few hundred subscribers — each issue, like this book, containing my poems with my wife's drawings.

Sally, our cat, is furious with me for writing a DOG book that hardly mentions her. I hope this makes it up to her.

Do cats give a damn about us — are they aware of us as more than cat food can openers and obedient hands? Do they feel "love" for us? I think so, but it's not always easy to detect. And until one has learned to tune them in, it's fascinating to observe how, as quickly as swift-blown clouds snuff a sunny day, a cat shifts from a cuddly or dignified friend to a ghoul to an icy vacuum — as fast as we can change our minds.

Thus, cats teach us the extent to which we create the world about us. The dog steadily presents us with our own image, while the cat dazzles us with intricate modulations from image to empty mirror — like the shimmer of an iridescent butterfly wing.

That's a cold paragraph: It examines cats much as we imagine cats examine us. I've learned to detect the person (?) in that twisty body — or have I been taken in by mirror magic? Cats are an exercize in daring to know what I know. With dogs, it's hard to UNknow the presence there of a being with an innerness much like one's own (though sociopaths and many psychologists overcome this difficulty). Cats are less embarrassed about not being human.

But here they are, with us, having become part of our humanness — or whatever it is we are. Some people are uncomfortable around cats, perhaps because they evoke such questions:

> I stroke Sally the cat, loving her, and yet
> I have more in common with Hitler, Stalin,
> a Klansman, a lawyer or even a psychiatrist
> than with this cat . . . or if not, who are we,
> really, you and I, Sally?

Final Note: The dedication omits my first cat, Midnight, who stopped at our porch for milk every day for months when I was five or six. Midnight was a silver tabby, but I liked the name, borrowed from radio's Buster Brown show (which, on TV, became "Andy's Gang"). The radio show starred "Smilin' Ed" (not Andy, but no less divine*) and his entourage, including the infamous Froggy the Gremlin (HIYA! HIYA KIDS!), a goldfish and a cat named Midnight, whose particular charm was that she had a one-word vocabulary, "Nice." Even when caught dabbling her paw in the goldfish bowl, her only response to accusation was (in a flat mincing falsetto) "Nice." Nice!

* "Andy's Gang" featured Andy Devine.

No Cats Have Been Maimed or Mutilated During the Making of this Book

...But Some of Them Are Disappointed — *DEEPLY* Disappointed — in Me

Wherever the cat curls up,
instantly
she has always been.

The cat looks right at me
and makes a decision,
but refuses to tell me what it is.

From the lawn two houses down a big red cat
spots me coming, uncoils ever so slowly,
moseys to the curb, vanishes beneath a car,
peers out from behind a front tire, looks away,
earning the Oscar for best performance
in “I Don’t Care About You — I Just Decided
It Would Be Nicer Here.”

White cat leaps
into the bushes . . . out floats
orange butterfly.

Cats look so knowing — but their skill
is not knowing, but being able to exclude
from their world all but the tiny scope
of their knowing.

One by one the cats leave us:
the black one who talked to us
plaintively when hungry, but wouldn't
be stroked, the mottled unfixed fellow
who might loll in my lap and luxuriate
against my fingertips or as readily
blaze up biting at any part that moved —
gone, both gone now, both missed,
all that presence so immiscible missed.

Along the sofa,
a sentence of cushions —
for period, this cat.

We twist in bed, the covers sticking,
winding to one side, then the other,
like a Torah, some Rabbi scrolling us
back and forth, searching for this week's
portion, which he must have found,
placing on it, for marker,
this cat.

Of her own volition the cat leaves my lap —
I can walk!

The cat's spinning eyes inches from mine
create tidal disruptions in my space,
but fail to tug my bare arms out
from beneath the covers (to make my
fingers available to scratch her head),
so she escalates, touching with gentlest
cloud-soft forepaw my beard,
then my lower lip, and I know
if I don't surrender my hands, next
from the cloud a tiny spark of lightning
will catch at my beard, then prick my chin . . .
you idiot cat, I'd better stroke your head
before I have to swat you!

"Wait — what's that
in her mouth! Don't let her in!"
Sorry, cat.

Sorry, sleeping cat : I've just got to
uncross my legs.

Downstairs she's saying
"No . . . no . . . NO!" What's that
cat doing now!

Almost indifferent to rebuff,
the cat whines, then off to lick herself,
such vigorous licking, perhaps
as a consolation.

I got teary reading about it:
Mother cat in New York carries her kittens
from a burning garage one at a time,
her picture in the paper, fur burnt off, eyes
blistered shut. Cats are so . . . scaredy.
But she went back into the flames again
and again until all her kittens were safe —
that's one hell of a maternal instinct!
What have we done to you, little fixed cat?

Low Though She Walks

The cat is my shepherd; always she wants.
She leadeth me downstairs to her food dish where,
though it is an easy jump for her,
she maketh me to lift her up,
or if I do not,

squawks her sour little squawk of want
repeatedly, the only sound more nagging
than a baby's whine, more hateful
than the juicy shploth shploth shploth
of a dog's tongue, ceaselessly licking himself
at 2:00 in the morning.

She greets me at the door and instantly begins
to lead me the way she would have me take her —
runs ahead, pauses to make sure I move with her,

and if not, insists with her swishing tail,
her flat cry of want.

When she would go out, she escorts me to the door,
sits facing it, all prim, shoulders snugly hunched,
forepaws daintily paired — Momma's little pet,
only the tip of her tail twitching,
her whole being become an arrow pointing at the door
as if to say OPEN HERE.

She is shepherd of hands as well as feet.
If she finds them otherwise occupied,
stubbornly she presses her small head against them
(wanting) until they drop their pens, remote controls,
spoons and forks, to stroke her —
and then they must stroke exactly the right place,
for when she's had enough on the skull,
she moves her delicate chin against fingertips,
sharply protesting cursory inattentive stroking
or too much or too little handling,
as hard to satisfy as a lover who hasn't yet told you
she's in love with another.

If hands ignore her (and perhaps she knows
it is we who move the hands), she lips them
ever so gently, so gently (raspy little touch
of tongue), then suddenly tiny teeth (we call it
a lovebite) cannot be ignored.

If, at night, when she wants to perch on my chest
and be stroked, I keep my hands under the cover,
she catches my eyes in hers, nudges forward until I feel
on the tip of my nose the cold wet electric touch of hers.

Then her face withdraws, she reaches out a tentative paw
to touch — barely touch — my chin,
the tentative paw sprouts less tentative claws and,
if I let the process escalate, I may be deeply touched.

If I roll her off, she is careful to slink away
across my pillow, pausing, tail high, to flaunt
an inch from my face her furry bottom,
then leap from bed to bed table,
where she paws a wristwatch or ring
to the floor, leaps after it and, with agile puck work,
knocks it into the most inaccessible under-bed cranny.

She is the shepherd, too, of laps and special spaces —
sheets of paper upon which she can sit, Sphinx-like,
or bags or boxes or shelves she can occupy —
and of attention, which she has determined the dog
shall not have, ever, to himself.

And if, turning to stone, we repulse all demands,
thoroughly thwart her, deaf to her cries,

thrust her aside (because we are busy and because —
O thank the Lord! — because we are much much
bigger than she is), then she strolls away,
stops to face us and lick herself,
long, tongue-stretching, rhythmic licks

(to tell us she doesn't give a damn?
to recover her cool? to make herself new and better,
more worthy of cuddling? to rid herself
of our now despised spoor? to release nervous energy,
as if puttering over housework?),

perhaps even assuming the drumstick-up,
        snout-down position
of industrial-strength crotch cleaning,
then settles on a cushioned chair and is instantly
asleep, a limp, tufted circle as undemanding
as the cushion, unimaginable that this tiny
silver-grey tigered ball of softness could ever loom
hugely over us, an insatiable maw of wanting.

Lightly touch her — she purrs against your touch,
such a good cat: She shall not want, no,
she shall never want.

That little, piercing wail, that feeling
that I'm guilty of something, though
I have no idea what — if the cat
spoke our language, she would say,
"I'm sick and tired of this life,
scratching my claws to the bone
day after day — and for WHAT!"
"WHAAAT!" she says. Mother, have
you come back to us as a cat?

Efficient cat: Two big bold eyes
and just enough of everything else
to keep the eyes going.

Fierce mama bird divebombs the cat —
matriocious!

Mounted Cats, Mounting Cats and Those Who Seek A Cat To Mount

Wiping out our rarest species,
White man trashes jungles — oaf he! —
Stuffing every tiger he sees —
What is left? A cat as trophy.

Oh no! Not another kitten!
Let our cats be fixed for no fee.
Even as these words are written,
We approach a catastrophe:
Tomcats vie, all hormone-smitten,
Each to win his cat-ass trophy.

On trails with turnings beyond count,
In canyons hymned by Ferdé Grofé,
If you should meet a catamount,
It might well mean a catastrophe.
Just stand still — don't run, don't taunt.
Maybe he'll leave his scat as trophy.

Strolling

Here I go walking down the street,
Pushing the sidewalk past my feet;
Lawns, children, leaves and sun —
These will go on when Dean is done.

Streets are just lines from me to you;
Cars find your door and poems too.
Lawnmowers, cats that watch me pass —
Curls of dream, dreamt by the grass.

Here I go walking down the street,
Passing dobermans on their beat.
"WOOF!" Do they think I'm good to eat?
"WOOF!" they reply and "WOOF!" repeat.

I move on. The jagged barking goes
Away; the wounds of silence close
(Motors rumble, birds go tweet —
I am the silence on this street).

Softly strolling down the walk,
But my head is full of talk;
See, the cats all stop and gawk:
"Don't think so loud — you'll spoil my stalk!"

There's the front page blowing down the street:
It's your whole world, all incomplete.
The headlines shrill: HEY! HEY! WE'RE HERE!
THE END OF EVERYTHING MAY BE NEAR!

The cat won't even twitch an ear;
Is she pretending not to hear?
Reliable sources hsst! and mutter,
Quietly blowing down the gutter.

Dreaming and dreaming down the street . . .
"Try," says the sidewalk, "to be concrete."
Leaves with my notions of leafdom meet:
"Try," say the leaves, "to be discrete."

Dressed up in wind and sun and stars —
"Look! He's all naked!" squeal the cars.
Here's a dead end, but I'll go on
From me to you when streets are gone.

The cat pokes her face into places,
thereby certifying them as places.

I want to write about something else,
but you are such a lovely cat!

"Here's a present," she says,
picking the cat off her lap and
plopping her onto my chest.
I mock-meow: "Ebenezer Blehert!
I am the cat of Marriage Present!"
The cat lifts her rump in my face
and hops off the bed.

Made to release her mouse,
the cat won't look at me.

Blessed is the cat, who forgives me
when I toss her soft unmoving gifts
into the woods.

The dog relishes licking my nose
with his big floppy tongue. Lucky the cat
has no such craving — her raspy tongue
would file my nose to a nub.

Home late. Three meowing cats
lead me into the kitchen.
Call Of The Tame!

Writer's Block

Some days I can't begin to write.
My pen cannot reach the paper,
blocked by an impervious presence —
the cat.

Two definitions of "perverse":
Not a penny; all my verse is free.
Or: The page of poetry in progress
upon which the cat perches to purr.

Trying to write;
the cat invades my lap —
her lap.

I hold my notebook over her,
but — "Squawk!" —
she's gone.

Now she won't look at me,
but soon I'll be, alas,
forgiven.

If only this sheet of paper
could attract poems as easily
as it attracts the cat.

Funny how a poem (like a house)
comes to life when a cat
peers out of it.

Easy to tell her
from the other cushions —
two pointy things stick up.

Touch them . . . twitch!
Whistle . . . they twitch! Touch almost . . .
but . . . not . . . quite . . . TWITCH!

Pestered, she stirs, ascends from and into her
hunched self like Dorothy's puddled witch
resurrected . . . frrrumps off the couch and
slouches away, not looking back,
stiff-haunched, sulking: "You've been
toying with me!"

Tabby Taboos

Cats are sacred in that land.
The worst curse befalls one who moves a cat
from where it has settled, a curse so vicious
that no decent citizen will associate
with known cat movers, lest they share
in the curse. Cat movers live and die
alone, feared, hated, whereas those who most
suffer the insouciance of cats are blessed:
For example, the sainted soldier bayoneted
when he would not join the retreat
because a cat had crept into his lap to sleep.
Or the writer who gave up on meeting a deadline
because his cat had settled on the manuscript.
Or the bride and groom, she all night
on her back, wakeful with the need not to turn, he
foregoing conjugal rights each night
of their honeymoon rather than disturb
the cat who settled on her belly.
Cats, it is believed, settle with such
confident complacency that to budge a cat
is to challenge cosmic inevitability
and perturb the heart of Grace. One who
inadvertently disturbs a cat (for example,
opens the front door to go out, causing

the cat — unseen — on the front step to unfold
and saunter away) can propitiate the universe
by penances, rich gifts for the neighborhood cats
such as spiced mice of elaborate design, hours
of community service — dangling shoelaces,
providing a steady lap, stroking and scratching —
but one who shoos or nudges or teases
a soft-breathing furpuff, for that one
is no recourse other than a celibate lifetime
dedicated to providing safe surfaces for the
sprawling, serpentining, stretching, scratching
and sleeping of homeless cats, whose encircled
slumber tunes the spheres.

Humans get tougher generation by
generation as only those savage enough
to brush cats (who refuse to understand
hints) off the bed — only they produce issue,
who, in honor of the cat's departure,
are called "offspring."

I'm going to eat the cat! I am! I am!
(The fat cat on the dining room table
doesn't budge, doesn't twitch a whisker,
doesn't believe a word of it.)

Grey cat
halfway across the street
tail high
hesitates

My mysterious feline,
she who MUST have her head scratched
is soon no mystery.

Think of them as people, all people, like us,
but different. Isn't it strange? There are
little furry people with tails and snouts,
cat people, dog people, mouse people, people
with feathers and wings, people with stingers
and antennae, tiny people we aren't sure we can
talk to, people we eat! I look out the front door
and there, prowling the flower bed, is an odd
pointy-eared person, hunch-shouldered, shy, in
striped grey pajamas, inspecting our weeds
(weed people?), and as I watch, a curious person,
not very tall, black suit with brown stockings,
pokes his long nose under my hand. I think he feels
all that I can feel, but can form only the simplest
conclusions to account for the most complex emotions,
all the confusion running out his tail. A tiny
winged person flits at the door screen, its eyes
(too small for me to see), perhaps, meeting mine.
We people persons know each other so little,
the others even less, as if we name things so as not to
know them, the more named (Black, woman, child, cat,
those long Latin names), the less known.

Somewhere in Beethoven

Somewhere in Beethoven, Opus 131: There's
a girl's face — detail from El Greco —
on one wall and another — Modigliani —
on another. There are three dogs
and a cat in the room. No one smiles.
It's too solemn even for the cat,
who sluggishly meanders out.

I planned to write, but nothing
is happening, except to the violins,
which are trying to get excited
about the walls.

I, too, would like to saunter off
to lick myself or slouch and slobber,
delighted endlessly with an old piece
of bone.

Let us be truthful, Beethoven,
El Greco, and readers: We're waiting
for her to get home.

Nothing is more reassuring than the constant companionship of a cat to one who merely SUSPECTS that others do not understand him.

Beethoven belabors the quiet afternoon, making what he can of gently swaying boughs outside and the cat licking her tail, music trying to make time make sense.

The cat asks to go out.
I let her out. It is my brief pleasure
to please. Would my fun be prolonged
if I could enjoy thwarting her,
since I could go on NOT letting her out
for hours? No, for her freedom lingers,
a subtle musk. Somewhere
she ripples through tall grass . . .

Perilous Prowl

When puss doth sneak,
the mice do squeak,
for mice feel finnicky
when puss is sinnicky.

"Shhh! The children will hear!" say adults,
just as children teach each other what not to say
around adults. Eventually, infested with privacy,
we shoo the cat, lest thoughts be overheard.

I go to the door and no one's there, only
a serpentine of cat at my ankles; I notice
wet grass, busily twisting trees and a sky,
none of which were there earlier when a human
face met mine. People devour surroundings.
Each of us must be stuffed with grass, trees, skies.

The alien intelligence,
having gathered all the data it needed
about the unsuspecting earthlings,
dismantled its cunningly disguised
mobile camera units overnight.
Next morning millions of earthlings
called out in vain: "Here, Kitty!
Here Kitty Kitty!"

The Hirsute of Sappiness

"Isn't da kittums CUTE!" —
Turning her suit hirsute.

From “On Not Dying”

Once, staring intently back at a cat,
suddenly I saw a human face
staring at a cat, saw from where
the cat’s eyes were, saw so clearly
I could see a cat’s face reflected
in the human eyes. It was a flash —
then I was seeing a cat flinch
and gallop full tilt from the room
as if she’d sensed (as cats do)
a ghost. Once, looking
at someone who looked at me
for a long time, I said to her,
“Your face just disappeared,”
and she replied, “I know.
So did yours.” Once, lying
beneath pine trees, looking up
along the tall trunks through
pinwheeling branches to the sky,
I found myself in the sky,
and I could see and know
and I was I. Once, after making love,
I knew what she would say
before she said it and what

I would reply and what she'd say
to that, and I saw her knowing
me know this and I started to say
and she said, we said
as I knew we would,
"I know."

We're guests. We have to share a narrow bed.
It's easy: We're used to twisting
carefully around sleeping cats —
we haven't the heart to move them —
two contortionists in a box
pierced by swords.

I know we live forever — we <u>must</u>
if only to be what can return
the cat's wide open green gaze.

The cat's rear rises
to meet my stroke . . . and is gone!
Was I not worthy?

Cat wants stroking. Her body becomes
a tongue that tries to lick me all over.

Strange house. Cat walking
toward the door sees me, stops with
forepaw curled in air.

He wasn't our cat, big red shaggy
tom, but we'd watched, bemused, as he
put out a patient paw at dive-bombing jays
as if to say, "Lay off, fellas!" One day,
from our apartment window, I saw him
settle down in the grass out back.

He tucked his paws under for a Sphinx-
style or brooding-hen catnap — or
whatever metaphor, none came near
saying what he'd settled for, because

the next day, I noticed he'd not
moved — sick? I went down into that
yard and towards him (He looked
at leisure, still), saying "Are
you OK?" Then I saw a fly browsing

over one eyelid and should have known
enough, but had to touch (he looked
so soft and comfortable and able
to turn and lick himself and look
bored, breeze lifting the red fur)

and feel the heavy thing that had
replaced him beneath the fur, stiff
as a log.

Don't Tell ME Nothing's Changed — I'm No Fool!

With age Sally the cat grows peevish.
Her meow has lost its upturned questioning,
its hesitations, become repetitive flat
demand — and worse, a demand I cannot meet,
because I don't know what she wants.

It used to be FEED me! Go OUT! Come IN!
PET me! Let me squat RIGHT here (atop my
paper, in a lap, in that cabinet . . .).
Now, often, nothing is quite it.
She hunches in the open doorway,
switching her tail while flies or icy wind
or dead leaves sweep into the hall.
She walks to the freshly dished-out glop
(her favorite), sniffs and turns away.

Even petting has become a torment.
Before if I stroked her head and chin
just so, she'd half-shut her eyes and settle
like silk into purring bliss. Now nothing is
quite right, nothing is ever enough:
If I stroke between her ears, she shakes
her head and nudges her chin against my hand.
If I stroke chin, she presents cheek, if cheek,

then neck or (good Christian cat) the other cheek.
If I stop, she insists, treading tiny claws
into my legs. I cannot seem to scratch
exactly where it itches.

When my lover loved another — and before
I knew — all our simple pleasures became
impossibly complex, no touch, no rhythm
or pressure of stroke or kiss quite
to her taste. Her orgasms, once as undeliberated
as a child's glow when opening an unexpected gift,
were snatched from me as booty with cunning,
effort and hissing teeth — as a rebounder
emerges from the melee, clutching the ball
in both hands, then yanks it right! left! right!
over the heads of opponents, signaling
MINE!

Sally the cat has no feral lover (she hardly
goes out now), nor the fixings for one, but she's old,
losing weight, stiff-jointed — no longer leaps
onto kitchen counters. Poems have called death a lover.
Some inner twinge nags her, clings to her as tightly
as love, signaling new needs that she understands
as little as we do. Soon we will have to let her go.

The first time the cat curls up
against me and falls asleep,
I am proud: See! I can be trusted!
(Children & animals loved him,
the biographies will say.)
After a few nights of dreams of coffins
(because I can't turn over in bed),
my biographers discover that I am
a rough, direct man who sometimes
regrets his violent impulses afterwards,
but doesn't lose sleep over them.

The kitten's on my lap,
poised to swat at whatever moves.
I can write so long as I don't
move the pen.

White cat on the path
sees me coming, scoots.
Lonely human.

The guardians know we will soon
reach the stars, but they spare us.
Hair-trigger monitors, just beyond the
earth's atmosphere, watch the earth's
aura, ready, at the first sniff of
rage, hate, despair to snuff us out.
Year after year we pass the test
because of our powerful friends,
who, despite our madness, hope we can be
educated. While our madness persists,
knowing we would only bite the hand
that feeds us, our protectors maintain
their discreet disguises: The cats,
staring and humming, beam a subtle,
steady carrier wave. The dogs use it
to envelop the planet with an aura
of loyalty, eagerness, and love.

Two strokes and she slops
on her back ("Take me! I'm yours!")
on the grass, purring.

It is hard to refuse a cat or dog or small child anything; they are so certain! The only argument that works is brute force. Adults are more civilized: You just wave a reason in their faces, stirring up all the self-doubts planted long ago by brute force: "Are you sure that's what you want to do?" ("I'LL TEACH YOU ONCE AND FOR ALL . . . !")

Secretive people lack secrets;
you can only hold tight to a few,
for secrets are like cats:
They don't like to be held long.
You have to clutch one in both hands,
taking care to keep its claws
away from your face and wrists.
I am willing to tell you anything,
letting my secrets come and go
as they will, so have a wealth
of secrets — perched on my lap
and shoulders, nudging my hand
to be scratched, more secrets
than I can give away if I try.

"Don't tread on me!" Early version
of American flag, with rattler,
also the motto of this bed, you
silly horny cat!

Paralyzed bird, legs crumpled,
feathers torn. Shooed cat crouches
nearby. I should have let her
finish it. Mourning dove, black-bead
eyes, head twisted back, stiff —
neck broken? No. Fast breathing.
Now I must help it. Its shocked eyes,
the cat's covetous eyes hold me.
Nothing I do is right.

After two days caged on the back porch,
the bruised bird is well enough to fly
into the woods. No thanks from the
bird, nor from the cat. But I'd
do it again. Chicken dinner last night,
good, but beyond recovery.

Click!

Here comes the cat
with a look in her eyes
as if to say: "I'm not an idea
for a poem. I'm a CAT."

Here comes my wife.
She doesn't mind being
an idea for a poem —
smile for the poet, that's a baby . . .
Click!

Grey cat eyes me from the grass.
Behind her belly up prick ears —
two more . . . two more . . .
Tense tiny heads turn
slowly to my passing.

An old gorilla strokes a black kitten.
He's lonely, say the zookeepers,
so they've given him the kitten
for company. This was on TV
right after news from Bosnia and Somalia,
this mountainous gorilla touching the kitten
so gently you could cry.

6 A.M. — the dreams begin to get interesting,
snatching and subsuming half-waking thoughts.
It's rating-sweeps time, as day competes
with night for my viewing. Body, old lump,
favors sleep and produces hectic spectaculars
and reruns of old favorites — hey! there's
my first lover! — but CLICK! and here's my
wife, red-eyed and thick-featured with waking,
telling me to get up NOW, then the cat,
next to my head, does a demanding number,
accompanied by a chorus of suddenly unsuppressed
bladder tingling — it's so REAL, man, it's an
EXPERIENCE, <u>MUST</u> viewing, it's got me now,
I'm hooked . . .

Our whining cat — as impatient as the IRS:
Tame and Tithe wait for no man.

Cats, of all dumb animals,
are the dumbest, because only cats
let on they think we humans
are idiots. The other animals
all play dumb, knowing they have
a good thing going, for, to keep them all
in the style to which they are
accustomed (dog food, hay, tons of
grain for rats and mice, leavings
for every wild thing), we spend
autumn days sitting in air-conditioned
offices, wearing tight ties.

On the sunny step
a furry egg hatches:
out peeps head of cat.

Cat snakes through the grass. Three starlings
sweep away, shrilly resenting her
insinuations.

Having to sit through bad poetry —
how easily our cat would stroll away.

Cat on the couch,
still as any cushion,
except, hanging from the edge,
the tail, <u>almost</u> still, just the tip
bends up . . . unbends . . . bends . . . unbends . . .
On the carpet, watching,
fascinated,
a cat.

Poetry says turn off that TV
and spend some time with me.
I say look, watching TV
is all I can do with this cat
on my belly, sticking her paw gently
in my beard to remind me I've
neglected to continue to scratch
her head. Poetry says if you
cared for me at all, you'd shoo
the cat and turn off the TV.
I say Shhh!

Why The House Cat Doesn't Hunt

Mice is nice,
but tuna is soona!

To the coyote, munching garbage and scrawny
hard-won rodents — and to other wild survivors,
cats and dogs are sell-outs: They saw
that man's the only winner on this planet,
and decided to be on the winning side, while
all the others were being eaten or exterminated.

But now it appears that man's way leaves
no winners, not even man. Perhaps our pets
were not traitors, but emissaries, for
their innocence makes me want to do better.

Sinister purring white Persian aloll the lap
of the exquisitely urbane chief of SMERSH
who has trained you to spit and hiss
at all others and who presses the button
beneath his desk to plunge screaming maids,
butlers and pesky kids through the infernal
hidden trapdoor when they disturb your naps
or complain of your slashing claws — you can't
fool me: I heard your interview with
Barbara Walters — In real life,
you're just a pussy cat.

All The Right Moves

You're a funny looking lady — long whiskers,
hairy all over, chinless, hump-backed, long in the
tooth, whiny . . . yet somehow the essence
of feminine.

If I hit the dog in anger,
he cringes, stricken as if by plague
or poison, and when forgiven,
he's a friend for life, everything wagging . . .
but not more obedient.

I don't know what happens
when I hit the cat in anger:
She gets even by not letting on,
and she snubs forgiveness,
turning away to lick herself.

The Vet says to have him fixed . . .
but he's not broken!

A spot of sunlight moves slowly
across the room, containing always,
like a performer who refuses to abandon
the limelight, this sleeping cat.

Cat curled up on my chest as I
drift off to sleep . . .
Morning, cat perched on my hip.
Did she go and return,
or ride me down sleep's twisting current
as a lumberjack rides a log?

Cat, down the blanket over Pam's sleeping
belly, pussyfoots.

I'm not rich, but I've left my cat
fixed for life.

Felix Domesticus

Big bed: room
for both of us or for
one small sleeping cat.

Perched on my belly
so peacefully —
sorry, Puss.

Gently nudged,
she nuzzles my hand
and doesn't budge.

Furry sphinx,
until we solve your riddle
we can't make love.

Easy to make the cat rise:
Just stroke from head
to tip of tail.

She arches up
against my hand, resettles
on my belly.

Lifted off (squawk!) . . .
You turn to me. She squeezes
between us.

Between your breast and my hand
probes a head
to be scratched.

Hard to resist
the tiny taut stroked head,
eyes squinched in "Don't stop!"

I slide my arm around you,
cat stretched out
at our feet.

Though careful with our feet
(Ummm! You feel good!), "Squawk!"
She plipplops to the floor.

Absence of cat:
"I know when I'm not wanted!"
(Ahh! That's nice!)

Somewhere in the room
she licks herself as we make
the fur fly.

Parsing Notice

Royally asprawl our bed:
Pretty cat, am I your subject?

The papers say she drowned her children
". . . as if they were kittens" — but who
would drown a kitten!

Moon Cat

A sullen star or two,
a chip of moon, cat
stealthily twining
the bare stone porch
with dreams of tall grass
rippling in no wind.

The cat wants to be scratched
more than the poem wants to be written.

“Scratch my head,” says the cat.
“Open the cat food cans. Serve us.
Why else were inferior creatures given
opposable thumbs?”

Like a shark’s fin,
among tables, footstools moves
the tip of the cat’s tail.

When Fred the cat wants to be fed,
he meows a meow like an irate quack
repeatedly, looking back as he leads me
downstairs to his bowl, talking right
to me until I feel I can speak cat,
though he's never told me the word for
thank you.

The cat prefers Pam's more stable lap —
female legs, trained to hold still,
never cross without care.

Cat curled on the lawn, tail stabbing down
like the dagger from a comic-strip balloon,
containing what the grass is saying.

They had their tomcat fixed, so now the bag
is out of the cat.

Spring. The cat vanished last Fall.
Dead? Bird song everywhere.
Dumb cat!

The TV remote control, number one
on our lap-loving cat's list of great inventions

SCAT, tummy, you fat sleek cat!
No more from me. I'll bet the neighbors
are feeding you.

One A.M. Roar, screech
of burning rubber, bruised silence.
Is the cat in?

Who set the cat for Snooze Alarm?
Ten minutes after she meows to go out
(at 6 a.m.), she meows to come in.

Fred the cat hasn't appeared for meals
two days now. He usually squawks
for his food and demands seconds. This
is not like him. I'm afraid he's become
something else, something not like him
at all.

After 2 1/2 days of being a fly-ridden
lump in the woods, a smear on the road,
and a hundred other pathetic pictures,
Fred the cat taps at the pane beside
our door and strolls in, demanding
his next meal, gobbles it down, and asks
to be let out. We're being used.
We should clobber him
with a rolling pin.

A tiny bit of night
ripples toward me, detaches
at my leg, purring.

We've lost a cat, but
look at the three fine moths
we've gained!

Republican or Democrat? Like determining
the gender of a new-born kitten.

Cats and women — the voice questioning
when the eyes know all the answers.

Out of the way, silly cat!
Her belly is *my* belly to lie on,
not the public lie-belly.

Cat extends paw, catches it
in the blanket, withdraws (infinitessimal
rip), each motion with its arch and reverse
arch, curl and uncurl of a wavelet.

The cat goes
from my lap toward the chair . . .
hell, she's back.

Down! Down!
(Wherein The Dog Gets Into Everything — Even This Book)

Wind chases leaves here, there,
back again, mostly skittered
over grassblades, sometimes lofted
into a short scary flight
feet or inches off the ground,

shuffling a few at a time . . .
then, FWHOOSH! —
the whole yard whirls in air . . .
settles, nothing where it had been.

We could tame this playful wind,
teach it to fetch, roll over, play dead,
tease the tense-arched cat,
ruffle our hair, turn the pages
of our book for us, cool our coffee,
leap for joy and lick our faces
when we return home,

but we'd have to house-break it
(NO, MUSTN'T MESS THE NEWSPAPERS!
BAD WIND! MOMMY JUST SET HER HAIR!),
wary of releasing our soft sprite

(whimpering at the window on gusty autumn days)
to romp and mate with rough
sand-clawed wild gales.

The cat pushes her head against my hand
to be scratched. I only pat her once.
She gives my wrist a gentle bite. I
scratch her head & chin. She sprawls
before me, lolls about, without letting
her head leave my hand. I stroke down
her back, right off the crooked,
twitching tip of her tail, but,
inexhaustible pitcher of cat, she pours
her purr back into my palm, head
following tail as seamless as milk. I
scratch & scratch until she says, "That
will be all now," that is, begins to
lick up the rest of herself.

The cat seems alien.
Then she dies — THAT'S alien.
Where is my friend?

cat
 caaaaaaat
  caaaaaaaat
   caaaaaaat
      Qat

Putting on my shoes —
quick! before she sees the —
POUNCE! —
l
a
a
a
c
e

A lady is singing about JEEEEEsus.
Her voice isn't bad, but I miss the harsh,
simple yawl of our cat.

Curled up in a circle —
how can one so complete unto herself
need and need and need!

To hear the world's most piteous sound,
step on a dog's tail.
To hear the world's most outraged sound,
step on a cat's tail.

Just The Cat

It's one of the great clichés of cinema:
Someone is escaping or infiltrating,
stumbles in the dark, then dives for cover,
holds his breath while one guard or goon
two steps from his hiding place says to another:
"I heard something," then a long pause,
a cat's meow is heard and Fritz tells
Willie, "It's just the cat" — what a relief!
We all know how noisy cats are — bumbling
flat-footed through our boudoirs, always eager
to make themselves known to, for example,
big louts with guns — you know how those
stalking predators are. But "JUST the cat" —
what is this "just" stuff? No wonder cats
don't go to movies!

I've seen how cats would make movies —
for example, I've seen one cat sitting
and looking off into space or seeming to
while contemplating the progress of digestion,
while yards away a younger cat
aimed herself like a slingshot at the elder,
in full ass-wiggling crouch, doing her final

countdown to launch when she heard
my step behind her, turned, agitated,
saw it was me and shushed me (she didn't
say "shhh!"; but it was a searching,
tail-twitching look, just a hint of
co-conspiracy, I like to think), then
returned to pre-pounce rituals and at last
took her shot — scared hell out of her target.

When she heard me behind her, I think
she said to herself, "I heard something,"
then turned, saw me, and said to herself,
"It's just the human." If so, that's only
poetic just.

Wild Dotes

Our cat was sowing her wild oats
When someone tore her fine fur coat —
Her only one, on which she dotes!
Please, Vet, sew our wild symbiote.

The dogs and cats scrabble at the door or stand
facing it, but the oldest cat
paws at the door knob.

Peeping out of my shoes
which is sillier — kitten's face
or behind?

What am I? I am that which,
if it were a body, the cat's ears
twitching beside me, the flicker
of yellow jackets amid clover,
those fallen petals, that butterfly,
that ant strolling over the edge
of the step, that tree aflutter with breeze —
all these and whatever else the day moves
would be gentle hands stroking me.

Sally's getting on. The last time
I tossed her away, she didn't land
on her feet. I'll have to be angry
more gently.

G.I. sniffs up just to see if anything's
happening (like popcorn, maybe?)
and from my lap darts Sally's slashing paw —
Sorry, old dog, this human is taken.

The Cats Who Go With Us

Once there were me and Pam and 2 dogs and
3 cats, a big family, it seemed, when we'd
walk the dogs, and all the cats, each conveying
in its own way, "I don't know these people,"
would go with us.

Our lean swift black mutt, G.I., dashes ahead,
lopes back, circles us, dashes ahead . . .
Our doddering near-deaf poodle, Wilson, lags,
meanders toward the curb . . ."WILSON!" Woken
from an autumn dream, he looks up, shambles
toward us. Fred's a shaggy hoary black male, boon
to weed and burr hitchhikers, his baleful glare
belying his docileness. He likes to lie on tummies,
purr mightily and gently tread — after all,
with such a motor, he expects to go somewhere.
Doglike, he trails along. Sam (whom Pam
calls Bandit) is unfixed, just out of kittenhood,
gray-white dappled, savage! He scampers ahead,
snakes behind a parked car and waits
to pounce out upon our sleek, demure, insatiably
cuddly silver tabby, Sally, who's been a snarling
nervous wreck since Sam showed up.

(I'd thought it was a bird cheeeeeeping, trapped
in the downstairs hall. No bird . . . scrabbling behind

the door of our tenants' basement apartment.
I open the door: Out plops two inches of blotchy
gray and white kitten, all eyes and paws. I sit
on the stairs, let it come to me in tiny flops —
up my shoe, and, clinging by needles, my pants,
shirt — how cute! — at last, probing with
softest, gentlest furry face — OUCH! — it bit
my nostril hard.)

How odd — all these creatures parading along with us,
having so little and so much to do with us
and with each other. Pam and I, by general consensus,
are special, vertical dogs. That is, to the dogs
we're top dogs — or they are admiring humans —
while cats are alien. And the cats agree —
dogs and humans are lumped together in otherness,
except sometimes the cats confuse — not us, but
our hands, our warmth, our breathing with
some intimate possession, perhaps "mother."

When we don't do what the cats want,
but brush them away roughly (to discourage
their persistence), in their elaborately casual
sauntering off to auto-lingual preoccupation,
I sense befuddled hurt as well as resentment,
as if a toyed-with near-dead mouse should
strike back, then streak away. How often
I catch myself yielding to cat demands

(Scratch me just there! More!) lest they
hurt me with their silent disappointment.

It's easy to slam the door at Mom when she's
bitching and carping, harder when she sobs,
almost impossible when she goes stone silent
and looks right through you. So it is
when I disappoint a cat.

If ever we please them, they don't say thanks
in any language we can understand. If we displease,
they keep their forgiveness a secret, but
here they are — going with us (pretending
not to) around the block, a straggle
of alertly crooked tails.

Now there's just me and Pam and silver-tabby Sally.
The others have gone away to cat-and-dog colleges,
marriages, careers in Canine Communications Science
and Feline Foreign Relations — they phone on holidays.
Sally's old, no longer frisky, no longer so sure
she's not one of us: How piteously she meowed
after us when we walked too fast, leaving her
behind (before we heard her yawl) on the path —

just one little cat, but oh my, how much attention
and admiration she can absorb! With the loss
of nearly all our horde, we expected an unwanted

silence, a loss of presence, but no, each creature
is an infinite attention sponge, each tiny
sleeping blob of fur a limitless excuse
for the projection of our worlds,
the investment of our own passion and scope —

not that her inner life is unreal, no,
for the life we grant IS life — even dolls and cars
acquire expressive faces and talk back to us
as soon as we give them names;
and all that we invest in her she reinvests
in us with substantial return of interest:
We are her inventions as much as she is ours.
No wonder it hurts us when we disappoint her;
she pretends we don't exist, locking us away
from part of ourselves.

Sally will be going soon. We'll all go soon,
Pam, me, you, all those who go
with us.

His Eyes, His Glittering Eyes

Our new house was 20 miles out.
Sam, the young Turk of our cats,
had never been in car or carrying case.
No soothings, no "It's AWWWlright," no strokings
sufficed. It took both of us to engineer him
into the large cardboard case (paws catching
where they could).

Why I heard nothing from the back seat
I don't know. When we arrived, I opened
the back door and saw two eyes maniacally
glittering from a ragged hole chawed
and scratched through thick cardboard . . .

Before I could grasp what I was seeing, Sam
surged through the hole, past my fumbling hands,
out the open door and away, across neighboring yards
and easement — gone. I ran after, yelling "Sam! Sam!"
Hours later Pam and I crackled through November burrs
and briars, yelling "Sam! Saaaaam! Sam!"
We put up posters. There were high-speed,
cat-smearing parkways nearby, and at night,
from the woods, hoarse barking of foxes,
but we knew Sam was too ornery to be dead.
(Our other cats relaxed — no longer needing
to guard their tails, food bowls and dignity.)

Months later Pam saw him on a lawn, but the lady there
insisted she'd had "Roger" for "at least a year".
We've met him on local paths, fat and regal now.
He keeps his distance, pretends not to know us.

We'll never know if he knows or CAN know
we weren't planning to imprison him in that box
forever, just for the one short trip — or,
if he knew, whether it would matter: How long
is a cat's "forever"? I'm stuck with those
glittering eyes, their diamond-hard decision.
I don't like who I was, will always be,
in those eyes. But it's worth it,
being the villain, to have seen who HE was
at that instant, ready to do
whatever he had to do in his burst
to freedom.

INDEX

About the author:

Dean Blehert lives with wife, Pam, and cat, Sally, in Reston, VA. He publishes his own poems in his poetry letter, *Deanotations* — to which a few hundred readers subscribe — and has had poems published in, among others, *Kansas Quarterly Review*, *Crosscurrents*, *Bogg*, *Visions*, *Lip Service*, *Gold Dust*, *Dark Horse*, *Modern Haiku*, *Carousel*, *Light*, *Orphic Lute*, *Brussel Sprouts*, *Stroker*, *Carousel*, *View From The Loft*, *The Listening Eye*, *HWUP* and *New York Quarterly*.

About the illustrator:

Pam Coulter Blehert, besides illustrating Dean's poems, is a fine artist (oil, acrylic, water color, etc.) who has won numerous prizes (including Best of Show) in local and national juried shows and is represented by several galleries nationwide.